CPSIA information can be obtained
at www.ICGtesting.com
Printed in the USA
LVHW091721061019
633321LV00003B/680/P

9 781688 190108